Oboe Student

by Blaine Edlefsen
in collaboration with James Ployhar

To the Student

Level III of the Belwin "Student Instrumental Course" is a continuation of Levels I and II of this series or may be used to follow any other good intermediate instruction book. It is designed to help you become an excellent player on your instrument in a most enjoyable manner. It will take a reasonable amount of work and CAREFUL practice on your part. If you do this, learning to play should be a valuable and pleasant experience.

To the Teacher

Level III of this series is a continuation of the Belwin "Student Instrumental Course", which is the first and only complete course for individual instruction of all band instruments. Like instruments may be taught in classes. Cornets, Trombones, Baritones and Basses may be taught together. The course is designed to give the student a sound musical background and, at the same time, provide for the highest degree of interest and motivation. The entire course is correlated to the band oriented sequence.

Each page of this book is planned as a complete lesson, however, because some students advance more rapidly than others, and because other lesson situations may vary, lesson assignments are left to the discretion of the teacher.

To make the course both authoritative and practical, the books in Level III are co-authored by a national authority on each instrument in collaboration with James Ployhar.

The Belwin "Student Instrumental Course" has three levels: elementary, intermediate and advanced intermediate. Each level consists of a method and two or three supplementary books. Levels II and III each have four separate correlated solos with piano accompaniment. The chart below shows the correlating books available with each part.

The Belwin "STUDENT INSTRUMENTAL COURSE" - A course for individual and class instruction of LIKE instruments, at three levels, for all band instruments.

EACH BOOK IS COMPLETE IN ITSELF BUT ALL BOOKS ARE CORRELATED WITH EACH OTHER

METHOD
"The Oboe Student"

For Individual
or
Oboe Class Instruction.

ALTHOUGH EACH BOOK CAN BE USED SEPARATELY, IDEALLY, ALL SUPPLEMENTARY BOOKS SHOULD BE USED AS COMPANION BOOKS WITH THE METHOD

STUDIES AND MELODIOUS ETUDES

Supplementary scales, warm-up and technical drills, musicianship studies and melody-like etudes, all carefully correlated with the method.

TUNES FOR TECHNIC

Technical type melodies, variations, and "famous passages" from musical literature for the development of technical dexterity.

OBOE SOLOS

Four separate correlated solos, with piano accompaniment arranged by Blaine Edlefsen:
Allegro from the Divertimento No. 3 . . . . *Mozart*
Song of India . . . . . . *Rimsky-Korsakov*
Romance No. 1. . . . . *Schumann*
Piece in G Minor . . . . *Pierné*

How To Read The Chart

When more than one way to finger a note is given, the first fingering is the one most often used. The other fingerings are used in special situations.

● — indicates keys to be pressed.

○ — indicates keys which are not pressed.

On the **Full Plateau** oboe, the A, G, and D keys are perforated plates (perforated plateaus) which remain depressed during the trills $a\sharp^{1-2}$- b^{1-2} and $a\flat^{1-2}$- $b\flat^{1-2}$, $g\sharp^{1-2}$- a^{1-2}, and $d\sharp^{1-2}$- e^{1-2} to compensate for the sharpness of the upper note of these trills. These particular trills are very well in tune and fingered comparatively easier on this oboe model. **Ring Models** have ring keys in place of the perforated A, G, and D plates. As a consequence the upper note of the trills mentioned above are very sharp (the $a\flat^{1-2}$- $b\flat^{1-2}$ a full ½ step sharp) if the same **Full Plateau** fingerings are used. **Modified Plateau** models may have plateau keys with or without perforations. Perforated plateaus on these models, however, do not often function as pitch compensators but are on the oboe simply to make closing the holes easier.

It is important to consult the trill chart for all trills until they are thoroughly learned.

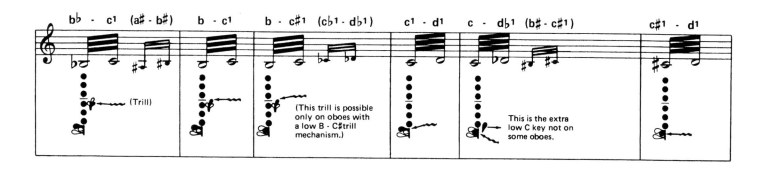

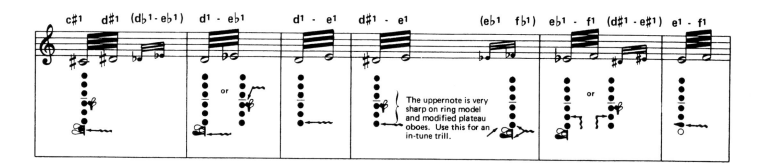

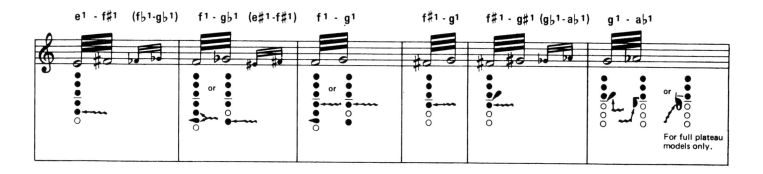

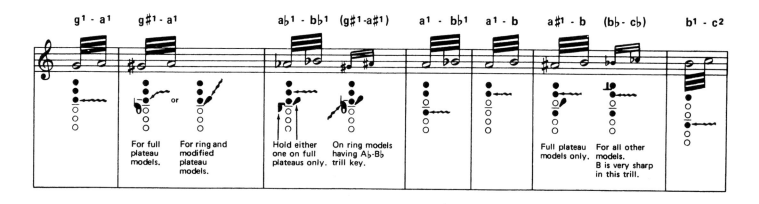

4

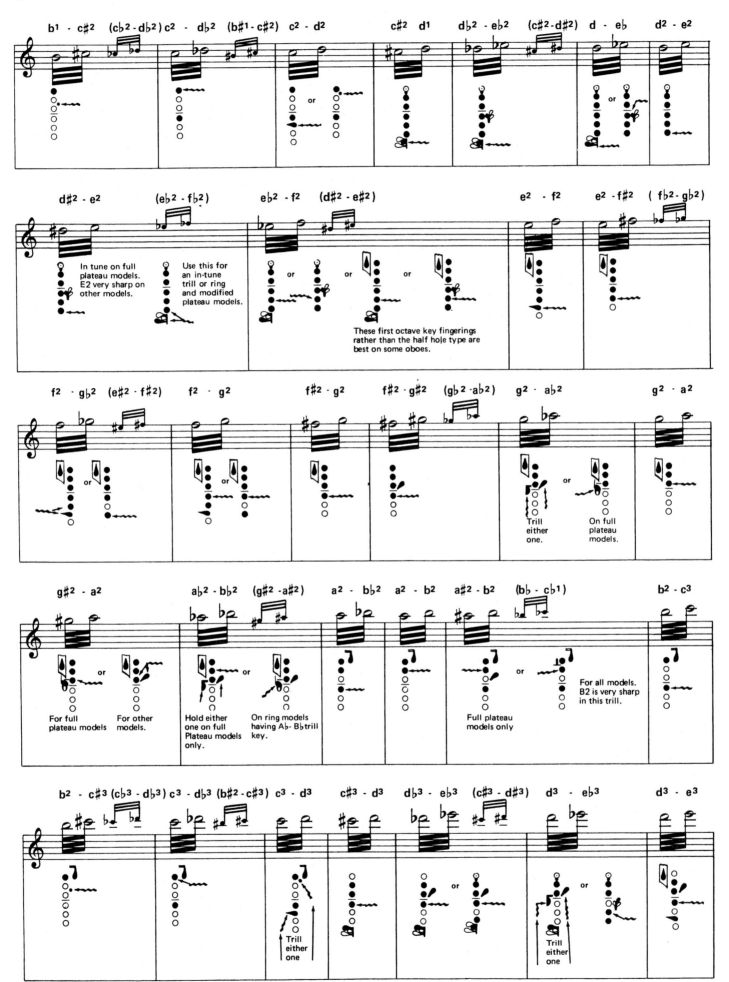

Daily Warm-Up Exercises

The following short Daily Warm-Up Exercises are designed to be the first ones the oboist should study and perform each day. Five minutes at a minimum each day on these exercises will help keep your fingering, tonguing, and embouchure in top performing condition.

Daily Warm-Up Studies For Half Hole And Octave Key Movements

HALF-HOLE MOVEMENTS

1ST OCTAVE KEY MOVEMENTS

COMBINING HALF HOLE and FIRST OCTAVE KEY MOVEMENTS

2ND OCTAVE KEY MOVEMENTS

COMBINING 1ST and 2ND OCTAVE KEY MOVEMENTS. Use only one octave key at a time.

COMBINING HALF HOLE and 2ND OCTAVE KEY MOVEMENTS'

Daily Staccato Warm-Up Exercises

Each day, choose two of the following rhythm patterns, one from each line, and apply them to the scale in ⑨ below, or apply them to any scale you know on pages 38 - 44 of this book.

Daily Loudness Warm-Up Exercises

Each day, choose one of the following loudness patterns and apply it to the notes in ⑨ below. Vary the key signatures.

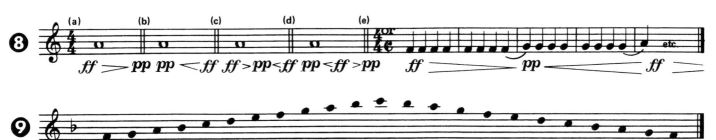

Scale Study In C Major

1 Allegro

2 ($\quad$ = 120) Legato Tonguing (as long as possible)

3 ($\quad$ = 120) Staccato Tonguing (slightly separated).

4 ($\quad$ = 120) Pay close attention to the tone length marks.

5 *Forked f (F) and Regular f (F) Study

R F R F R F R F F F F F R.

*If your oboe has a left hand f key, re-study ⑤ using the left hand f fingering instead of forked f.

Gopak

RUSSIAN

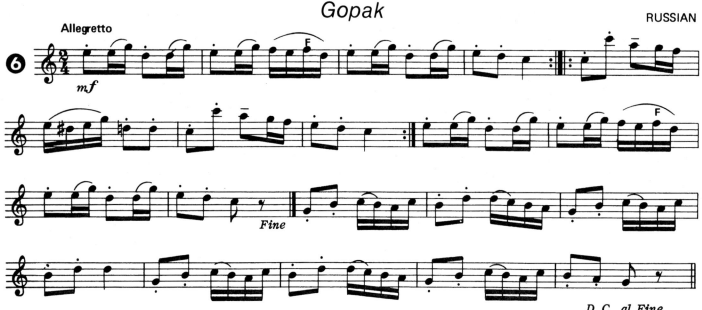

6 Allegretto

mf

Fine

D.C. al Fine

If you have not already done so, please see the book "STUDIES AND MELODIOUS ETUDES FOR OBOE" Level III, for more scale and technical studies which correlate with Method Book III.

A Minor (Harmonic Form)

Study In A Minor

BARRET

*These ornaments are called turns or gruppettos.

8

Each day be certain to WARM-UP on the exercises on page 5.

F Major Scale

F Major Scale in thirds.

F Major Arpeggio

Study In F Major

JOSEPH SELLNER

Important Embouchure Placement Studies

In oboe playing we must learn to set the embouchure for each note we play.
The general rules to follow are these:

1. Keep excess saliva from the lips and reed at all times.
2. The higher we play, the more we must roll (Do not slide or slip) the reed into the mouth.
3. The lower we play, the more we must roll (Do not slide or slip) the reed out of the mouth.
4. To maintain the same loudness level, blow less hard for the lowest note of a wide interval.
5. Blow harder for the highest note of a wide interval to maintain the same loudness level.

Follow the slurs exactly.

Valse Caprice

ANTON RUBINSTEIN

Lively waltz tempo

Please see the book "TUNES FOR OBOE TECHNIC", Level III, for more melodies which provide further technical development.

Playing High D (d³)

Sharp pitch and/or poor response are often characteristics of high d (d3); therefore if the first fingering does not work, try each of the others in turn to see which works best for you. The fingering for d3 is based on the low g1 fingering, the half hole for d3 serving as a kind of octave key; Note that depressing the low c key also lowers the perforated e key. Make certain that the e key is completely closed or a sharp pitch will result. Clean out the perforation in the e key if d3 does not speak easily. On the other hand, if d3 does not speak in slurred (or tongued) passages, lift the first finger left hand completely off the b key for the octave key effect. If d3 is then too sharp, you may depress either the e key or both e key and the d key to lower the pitch.

Tongue first, then slur. Repeat each measure until clean.

Rhythm Practice: Count in your mind as indicated below the staff.

Wondering

SCHUBERT

Playing High c♯ (c♯ 3)

The fingering for c♯3 is based on low f♯. The raised b plate (1st finger left hand up) serves as a kind of octave key. As in the d3 fingering, be certain that the low c key also closes the perforated e plate completely, or a sharp pitch will result. A sharp pitch may be lowered by adding the e key with the middle finger right hand.

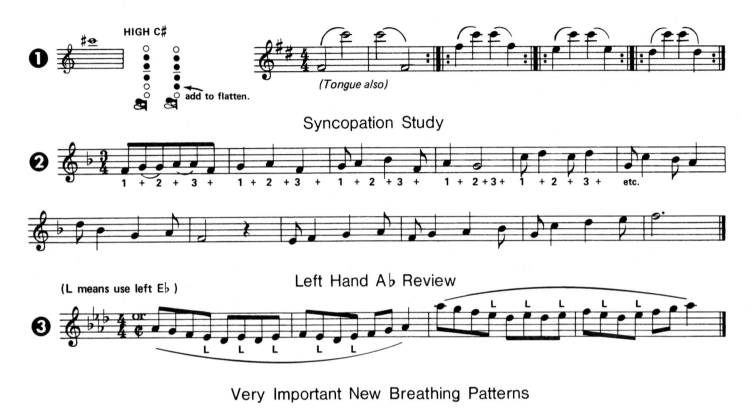

Syncopation Study

Left Hand A♭ Review

Very Important New Breathing Patterns

In oboe playing, letting air out (exhaling) at breathing places is important in order to maintain a low carbon dioxide level in your body. In the solo, Panis Angelicus below, follow the breathing places exactly until you can play comfortably from the beginning to the end without stopping. Later you may establish your own breathing patterns. o means let air out (exhale); i means take air in (inhale). Through careful practice you will learn how much to exhale each time. Inhale deeply each time.

Panis Angelicus

FRANCK

Review the list of correlated solos listed on page one. These solos, written specifically for this course will enhance the study of your instrument. We suggest that you supplement each of your lesson assignments with one of these solos.

D Minor *(Harmonic Form)* **Tongue, too.**

D Minor Arpeggio

The Wild Horseman

ROBERT SCHUMANN

Allegro

mf (Practice the whole piece staccato, too)

Fine

D.C. al Fine

Thanksgiving Hymn

For Review of Left Hand E♭

Tango

ALBENIZ

Andantino

Watch the rhythm and breathing patterns very carefully.

Study In B♭ Major

JOSEPH SELLNER

B♭ Scale in Thirds. Pay very close attention to the fingerings for low F and E♭.

Play the upper B♭ if your oboe has no low B♭ Key.

Loudness Study. Learn as written, then re-study tonguing each note two times.

Voices Of Spring Waltz

JOHANN STRAUSS

Waltz tempo

Study In G Major

Passages To d³ From The Second Octave Key Notes

Syncopation Study

Tonguing Study

Practice these rhythm patterns on various scales you know (C, G, B♭ , E♭ , for example).

Andante

MOZART

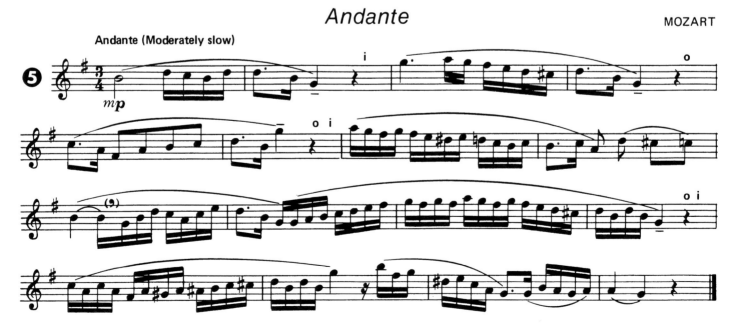

E Minor Scale

Thirds

Arpeggios

Study In E Minor

Allegro

Octaves Study. Learn two ways: First, top slurring; second, bottom slurring.

A Media Noche

JOSE AVILES

Slowly

mp

(Watch the counting)

Count: 1 + 2 ++

Introducing High e♭³

E♭ Major Scale

E♭ Major Scale in Thirds.

Introducing ¹²/₈ Time

JOSEPH SELLNER

Count: 1 + + 2 1 + 3 + + 4 + +

Loudness Study

Practice at a different tempo each day.

1st time – *pp* *p* *mp* *mf* *f* *ff* > *p* *simile* - - - - -
2nd time – *ff* *f* *mf* *mp* *p* *pp* < *f*

Bagatelle

Leggiero (Lightly - in 3 fast beats)

FRANCOIS COUPERIN

p (Work the breathing patterns out very carefully, especially on the D.C. Mark the patterns yourself.)

Fine

mf

D.C. al Fine

A Tied Note Study

An Important Tonguing Study

In this study, do not "clip-off (shorten) the last note of the slurs. On the contrary, play them full value as indicated by the dash as a reminder. To begin practice very slowly, then increase the Tempo to ♩ = 120. Practice the same pattern on other scales, too.

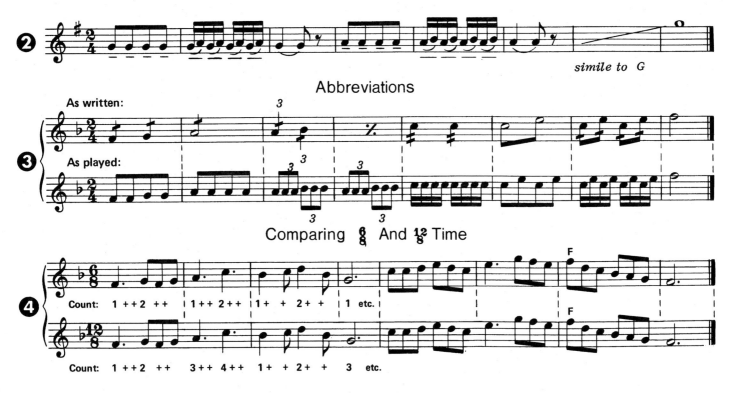

Abbreviations

Comparing ⁶⁄₈ And ¹²⁄₈ Time

Andante Cantabile

TSCHAIKOWSKY

Watch the breathing very carefully. Breathe exactly as marked for discipline.

*(i) indicates an optional breathing place.

Interpretation Of Ornaments In Baroque And Classical Music

Much of the music oboists play was written between 1700 and 1800, during the creative times of Bach, Teleman, Mozart, Haydn, and the young Beethoven. Trills and a variety of appoggiaturas are typical Baroque - Classical ornaments presented in this method.

The Long Appoggiatura ♩, ♪, ♬

The long appoggiatura appears in the music as a very small note, usually an eighth or a sixteenth note, followed by the main note of regular size. The general rule for the length of this appoggiatura is to take half the value from the main note; however, if the main note is dotted, that is, divisible by three, the appoggiatura receives two-thirds of the time value. The appoggiatura is always played on the beat and always slurred to the main note whether indicated or not.

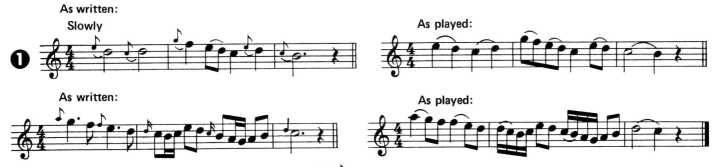

In more rapid passages, one of these same small notes (♪♬) indicates a short appoggiatura which is to be played one-fourth or less of the value of the main notes.

A Review Of c♯

Counting Study

Pay particularly close attention to the notes marked staccato (·)

Silver Wreath

TRADITIONAL

B.I.C.321

18

G Minor Arpeggio

Study In G Minor

Allegro

A Review Of c♯3 And d3

Accent Study

Slowly. Put very little tongue on the reed to make these accents. They should not sound percussive.

Loosen the lips at the beginning of each accent, then tighten the lips to diminuendo to piano.

KOWALSKI

Etude

Moderato (Watch the tied notes carefully)

* ⸴ indicates a good breathing place.

D Major Scale

Review exercise ③, page 18, before practicing this scale.

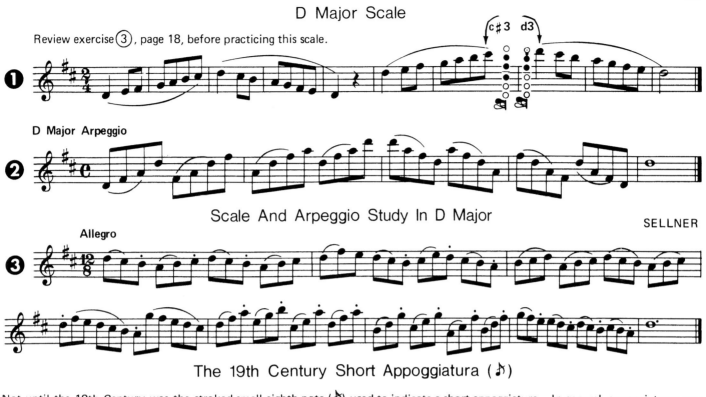

D Major Arpeggio

Scale And Arpeggio Study In D Major

SELLNER

The 19th Century Short Appoggiatura (♪)

Not until the 19th Century was the stroked small eighth note (♪) used to indicate a short appoggiatura. In general, appoggiaturas one half or one whole step away from the main note are played very short and on the beat. Appoggiaturas occurring at wider intervals from the main note are played very short and just before the beat.

Slurring And Wide Interval Study

Roll the reed out for descending intervals; in for ascending ones.

D Major Study

Ab Major Scale

1

Ab Scale in Thirds

2

Play this c with the flat part of the finger, then tip the ball of the finger to the Db Key for Db .

Ab Arpeggios

⁶⁄₈-³⁄₈ Rhythm Study

Play at a comfortable tempo

3

Chromatic Study

Practice 3 ways: ①as marked; ②all slurred; ③all tongued.

4

Study In Ab Major

means play right Eb first, then switch to left Eb so you will be able to play the following Db correctly.

R-L

5

The Standard Post-Baroque Trill (after 1800)

The trill is a musical ornament consisting of the rapid alternation of a given note and the next note above in the existing key. The interval may be a half or a whole step. If an accidental accompanies the trill sign, the upper tone is altered. Faster tempos require fewer alternations. Play the first note of these trills slightly elongated as indicated.

Trill Study

Study In F Major

SELLNER

Etude

Triumphal March From The Opera "Aida"

VERDI

D.S. al Fine

C Minor Scale (Harmonic Form)

Thirds

Study In C Minor

(Hold the tied notes the correct length.)

Count: 1 + 2 + 1 + 2 + 1 + 2 + 1 + 2 + 1 + 2 + etc.

Dotted Eighths In 6/8 Time

First learn in six beats per measure, then in two beats per measure.

Count: + 1 + + 2 + + 1 + ÷ 2 + + 1 + + 2 + + 1 + + 2 + +

1 + + 2 + + 1 + + 2 + + 1 + + 2 + + etc.

Fine

D.C al Fine

The Wild Horseman
(In C Minor)

SCHUMANN

Allegro

mf

(Practice the whole piece staccato, too.)

Fine

D.C. al Fine

Termination Of Trills

Trills are very often finished (terminated) by adding a complimentary note just before the last note of the ornament. This added note is in the existing key and one scale step below the main note. Notice that this lower note replaces the upper note of the trill at that point.

Study For Fast Staccato

ITALIAN PEASANT DANCE
TRADITIONAL

Rhythm And Tonguing Studies

Sing the tonal symbols (tudub like toodoob) in rhythm before practicing on the instrument. Play each study on a different scale at each practice session.

Serenade

Moderately slow. You must count as indicated.

SCHUBERT

24

A Major Study

Fingering #2 for low B.

Oboes which have no low B - C# trill mechanism require fingering #1 for low B.

Thirds

Arpeggio

c#3

Scale Study In A Major

A dot equals half the value of the preceeding rhythmic symbol; hence the second of two dots in a row equals half of the value of the preceeding dot.

As written: As played: As written: As played:

1+2 + 3 +4 + +   etc.   1 +2 + 3 + 4 +   etc.   1 + 2 +3+4 +   etc.   1 +2 +3 +4 +   etc.

March Pontificale

GOUNOD

Allegro (March style)

Count: 1 + 2 + 3 + 4 +   1 + 2 + 3 + 4 +

Allegretto — Pay attention to the staccato notes.

A Review: c♯3 , d3 , e♭3

Study In A♭ Major

"While Kedron's Brook" From The Oratorio Joshua

HANDEL

B Minor (Melodic Form)

Fingering 2 is for oboes with low B - C# trill mechanism only.

Thirds

Arpeggio

Study In B Minor

Suggestions for Further Study: Throughout 1 and 2 above, you may hold down the c-pad spatula key with the first finger, left hand (see fingering chart, page 2). This fingering makes the notes c2 and c3 impossible to play, yet all the other notes are not affected. Passages between a# and b are consequently very smooth since no c's can be played accidentally between these two notes.

§/§ Rhythm Study

Slowly, in two beats.

Count: 1 + 2 + + 1 + + 2 + + 1 + + 2 + + 1+ + 2 + + 1 + + 2 + +

1 + + 2 + + 1+ + 2 + + 1 + + 2 + + 1+ + 2 + + 1 + + 2 + +

Canzonetta

TSCHAIKOWSKY

Andante

mp (Breathe where marked; i = air in; o = air out.)

Count: 1 + 2 + 3 +   1 + 2 + 3 + 1 +2 + etc.

*(9) denotes possible breathing places.

Rhythm Study

C - D Trills

C - D Trill Keys The c2 - d2 or c3 - d3 trills are executed by adding one of the C - D trill keys to the regular c fingering. The right hand c - d trill key seems more useful than the left one which is not made on some student line oboes. Each key is played with a corresponding middle finger either at the ball or the underside of the middle joint.

B - C♯ Trills

B - C♯ Trill Key Use the ring finger at the ball or at the underside of the middle joint.

Rhythm Study: In Place Of

Use C - D Trill Key here.

Use C - D Trill Key

Etude

Moderato

Write out the counting.

Fine

D.C.al Fine

Baroque And Classical Trills (circa 1700-1800)

Trills written during this period almost without exception began on the note above the written trill. They usually required a termination, the half trill and certain continuous trills being notable exceptions. In addition, the first note of Baroque trills usually requires the regular fingering (see the trill section, Lesson 24). The trill must begin on the beat, not before.

The music by Bach, Handel, Telemann, Vivaldi, Haydn, Mozart, and the young Beethoven is of this period.

Trumpet Voluntary

JEREMIAH CLARKE
(c - 1673 - 1707)

A Study For Rhythm And Tonguing Style And Discipline

Sing the tone symbols first to learn the articulation.

Chromatic Study

Db Major Scale

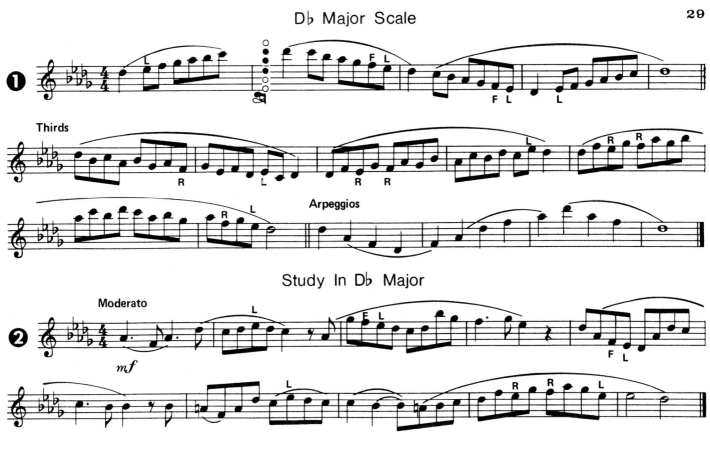

Thirds

Arpeggios

Study In Db Major

Moderato

mf

General Rules For Trilling

Passages between these notes: d2 - e2, d#2 - e2, eb 2 - f2, g2 - a2, g#2 - a2, and ab 2 - bb 2, ordinarily require the movement combinations of either the first octave key and half hole or the first and second octave keys. In fast trills, we do not make these movements. We simply retain for both pitches that octave key which is used for the lowest note of the trill. However, the first note of Baroque trills usually requires the regular fingering. In addition, sometimes on certain long trills the first few alternations may be slow enough to require the use of regular fingerings; thereafter the trill fingerings are used.

Trill the ring finger only

Trill middle finger only

N.B.*

On ring model oboes, use right Ab - Bb trill key if it is on your oboe.

Etude In C Major

Fast

N.B. * On some oboes, this fingering works best for the eb 2 - f2 Trill: ———(Trill)

F#Minor (Melodic Form)

Thirds

Arpeggio

Double And Triple Note Ornaments

Two and three note ornaments called grace notes, slides, and appoggiaturas may be played on or before the beat. In Baroque and Classical music, and even through Beethoven and much after, the double note ornaments were usually played on the beat.

As written:

Slides   **Disjunct Appoggiaturas**

As played:

Theme From The 7th Symphony

*BEETHOVEN (1770 - 1827)

Allegretto (♩ = 76)   Play on the beat

p dolce
[sweetly]

Loudness Study

f $p<f$ $p<f$ $p<f$ $p<f$ $p<f$ $p<f$ $p<f$

Tambourin

*JEAN PHILIPPE RAMEAU
(1683 - 1764)

In a lively two beats

R

f

Play on the beat

R   R

Fine

D.C.al Fine

From now on you must become aware of a composer's lifetime dates so that you can determine how to perform ornaments such as trills and various appoggiaturas (grace notes).

Staccato And Rhythm Study - Spanish Style

Play only the dotted notes staccato.

Playing The Left Hand Articulated Keys: Left A♭ - G♯ Or E♭ - D♯

To execute certain trills and passages we often use articulated keys.

⌐L⌐ or ⌐L⌐ means to hold down the relevant left A♭ - G♯ or E♭ - D♯ for all notes within the brackets.

Melody From "Repaz Band" March

LINCOLN

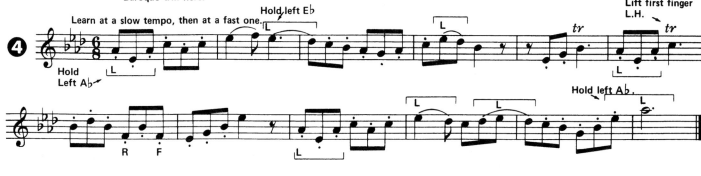

*If the g♯ pad does not completely close, tighten the screw on the closing f♯ key lever.
†If the E♭ - D♯ pad does not close completely, tighten the screw at the end of the E♭ - D♯ pad lever.

F Minor (Harmonic Form)

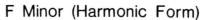

Preparing For High e³ And f³ Through Essential Fingerings In Lower Registers

If you can play all the exercises in ②, the fingerings for e3 and f3 on page 33 will be comparatively easy.

⌐L + L⌐ means hold both the left A♭ - G♯ key and the left E♭ - D♯ key down together.

Use the regular fingering for the first note of each type of trill.

Oboe Solo From The 4th Symphony

TSCHAIKOWSKY

Playing High e³ And f³

Things to Remember

1. Beginning with e3 we use the first octave key again.
2. For both e3 and f3 we retain the half hole fingering.
3. Blow harder and roll more reed into the mouth for these pitches.

Depress the left g♯ and d♯ keys with the little finger.

F Major Scale to f3

Be certain to roll the reed out of the mouth when descending, especially for the notes in this slur.

Pay attention to the accent (>).

Staccato Study

Chromatic Study

Nocturne

A. BORODIN (1834 - 1887)

Moderato

Play before the beat.

mf

Use C - D Trill key

Elongate these notes slightly

C - D Trill

34

*As in ②page 31, ⌐L⌐ means to hold down the D# - Db Key for all the notes within the bracket.
† This Adagio is a perfect work to practice using the left hand F key in place of all forked F's.

Trill Pitch-Compensators On The Full Plateau Conservatory System Oboe

Pitch compensators are the perforated plates A, G, and D, which remain depressed during the trills a♯1 - b1 and a♭1 - b♭1, g♯1 - a1, and d♯1 - e1 to compensate for the sharpness of the upper note of the trill. The trills an octave higher are the same except for the appropriate octave keys. See Trill Chart, pages 3 and 4 for the exact fingering.

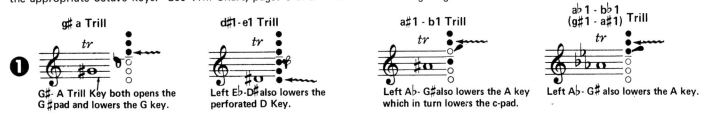

On ring model oboes and on certain plateau models without pitch compensators, these same trills must be fingered the following way to produce in-tune trills. See Trill Chart, page 3, for further explanations, and fingerings.

Passages In The High Register

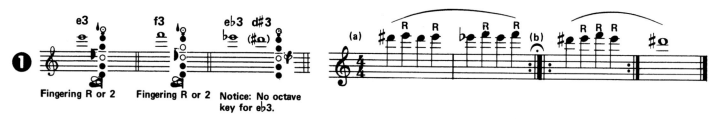

Chromatic Study To f³

Rhythm Study

Mexican Hat Dance

TRADITIONAL

Difficult Passages In B Major: A Preliminary Study

d♯1 - b: add b key and slide to c or c♯ key. For b - d♯1, reverse the movements.

d♯1 - b: lower left arm to play low b - key with middle joint and add low c or c♯ key. Move in reverse for b - d♯1.

b - a♯: leave finger on low b while tipping to low a♯ key. Reverse for a♯- b.

Scheherazade

N. RIMSKY - KORSAKOV
(1844 - 1908)

Fingered Scales, Stepwise And In Thirds, And Arpeggios

Definitions of Symbols Which Appear Above or Below Certain Notes And Passages.

F . . . . use forked - ƒ.

R . . . . use right hand f or use the related ab- g♯ and/or eb- d♯key(s)

L . . . . use the related left hand ab- g♯ and/or eb- d♯key(s)

⌐L⌐or⌐ L⌐ hold down the appropriate left ab- g♯ or eb- d♯key for all bracketed notes. Passages so marked must also be practiced without the brackets. Passages marked ⌐L⌐or⌐ L⌐indicated where either the left articulated ab- g♯ or eb- d♯ keys may be used.

⌐L + L⌐. hold down both the left ab- g♯ and eb - d♯ keys together with the left little finger for all bracketed notes.

1, 2, 3, or 4 refers to a specific fingering for that particular note. To learn the fingering, see the fingering chart, page 2. If no number appears above or below a note having numbered fingerings, fingering number 1 is recommended.

Chromatic Scale (Slur and then tongue all scales.)

C Major Scale

Thirds

Arpeggios in C Major

A Minor Scale (Harmonic Form)

Thirds

Arpeggios in A Minor

Practice with and without brackets.

F Major Scale

D Minor Scale (Harmonic Form)

B♭ Major Scale

Arpeggios in F Major

Arpeggios in D Minor

Play D if you have no low B♭ Key.

Arpeggios in B♭ Major

G Harmonic Minor Scale

Thirds

Play D if you have no low B♭ key.

Arpeggios in G Minor

E♭ Major Scale

Thirds

Arpeggios in E♭ Major

⌐L + L⌐ means hold both left A♭ and E♭ down together.

You must practice two ways:
1. ⌐L + L⌐   ⌐L + L⌐
2. ⌐L + L⌐

C Harmonic Minor Scale

Thirds

Arpeggios in C Minor

Practice with and without the brackets.

A♭ Major Scale

Practice with and without the brackets.

Thirds

Arpeggios in A♭ Major

You must practice two ways:
1. L + L   L + L
2. L + L

F Harmonic Minor Scale

Thirds

Arpeggios in F Minor

D♭ Major Scale

Thirds

Arpeggios in D♭ Major

42

G Major Scale

Thirds

Arpeggios in G Major

E Harmonic Minor Scale

Thirds

Arpeggios in E Minor

D Major Scale

Thirds

Arpeggios in D Major

B Harmonic Minor Scale

(Also practice all B Minor Scales and arpeggios with the c-pad spatula on throughout.

❶

Use fingering #2 for oboe
with B - C# trill

Thirds

Arpeggios in B Minor

Play e if you have no low
A# (B♭) Key.

For oboes with low B - C# Trill.

A Major Scale

❷

For oboes with
low B - C# Trill.

Thirds

Arpeggios in A Major

F#Harmonic Minor Scale

❸

For oboes with
low B - C# Trill.

Thirds

Arpeggios in F# Minor

Please Note: Practice with and without the brackets throughout this entire page.

E Major Scale

Thirds

Arpeggios in E Major

C# Harmonic Minor Scale

Thirds

Arpeggios in C# Minor

B Major Scale

(Also practice all B Major Scales and arpeggios with the c-pad spatula on throughout.)

For oboes with B - C# Trill Key.

Thirds

Arpeggios in B Major

Play e if you have no low A# (Bb) Key.

For oboes with B - C# Trill Key.

Notes

Notes

Notes

Musical Terms With Which You Should Be Familiar

The following words indicate the general tempo, or speed of a composition from slow to fast:

Grave . . .	Very slow, ponderous and solemn
Largo . . .	Slow and broad
Larghetto .	Slowly
Adagio . .	Slow and leisurely
Lento . . .	Slowly
Andante . .	Moderately slow and flowing
Andantino .	Slightly faster than Andante
Moderato .	Moderately
Allegretto .	Moderately fast
Allegro . .	Fast and lively
Vivace . .	Very fast, vivaciously
Presto . . .	Extremely fast

Dynamics refer to the degree of loudness or softness of tone. The following symbols are the more important dynamic markings:

pp . .	*Pianissimo*	Very soft
p . .	*Piano*	Soft
mp . .	*Mezzo Piano* . . .	Moderately soft
mf . .	*Mezzo Forte* . . .	Moderately loud
f . .	*Forte*	Loud
ff . .	*Fortissimo*	Very loud
sfz . .	*Sforzando*	Played with sudden force
fp . .	*Forte-piano*	Loud, then immediately soft

The following markings suggest a gradual change in volume:

Crescendo—Cresc. . . .	Gradually louder
Diminuendo—Dim. . . .	Gradually softer
Decrescendo—Decresc. . .	Gradually softer
Morendo	Dying away
Perdendosi	Dying away in sound and speed
◁	Gradually louder
▷	Gradually softer

The following markings indicate a change in tempo or speed:

Ritardando—Rit. . . .	Gradually slower and slower
Rallentando—Rall. . .	Gradually slower
Accelerando—Accel. . .	Gradually faster
Ritenuto	Hold back at a slower speed
A Tempo	Used following one of the above markings to "resume the original tempo".
Tempo Primo	Tempo same as the beginning

The following signs appear in nearly every composition we play:

♩	Staccato — short	*D. C.* — (Da Capo)	Go back to beginning
♩	Tenuto — sustained, broad	*D. S.* — (Dal Segno)	Go back to sign (𝄋)
⌒	Slur	⊕	Skip to Coda
⌒	Fermata — hold, give extra time	𝄪	Double sharp
⁒	Repeat preceding measure	♭♭	Double flat
♩	Accent — play with force	*8va* — (Ottava) . . .	Play an octave higher than written

Words That Suggest Musical Style:

Ad Libitum (ad lib.) . .	At liberty		*Giocoso*	Playfully, gaily
Agitato	Agitated		*Grandioso*	With grandeur
Alla Marcia	In a march style		*Grazioso*	Gracefully, elegantly
Animato	More animated		*Legato*	Smooth and connected
Appassionato	With passion		*Maestoso*	Majestic, dignified
Bravura	With boldness and spirit		*Marcato*	Marked with emphasis
Brillante	Brilliant and sparkling		*Pomposo*	Pompously and dignified
Cantabile	In a singing style		*Scherzando*	Playful, jestingly
Dolce	Sweetly		*Sostenuto*	Sustained
Espressivo	Expressively		*Tranquillo*	Quietly

Other Common Words You Should Know:

Accidentals . . .	Sharps, flats and naturals not in the key signature		*Molto*	Very, much
Arpeggio . . .	Notes of a chord played separately		*Mosso*	More
Attacca	Continue with little or no pause		*Opus*	A musical work
Cadenza	A solo passage played with freedom		*Poco a poco* . .	Little by little
Divisi	Divided parts		*Quasi*	In the style of
Embouchure . .	Mouth muscles used in controlling the tone of a wind instrument		*Segue*	Proceed in the same style
Enharmonic .	Same in pitch but different notation		*Senza*	Without
Fine	Finish, the end		*Simile*	Play in a similar manner
L'istesso . . .	The same		*Subito* . . .	Suddenly, without pause
Loco	As written		*Syncopation* . .	When the accent falls on the weak beats
Meno	Less		*Tacet*	Be silent, don't play
			Tutti	All together